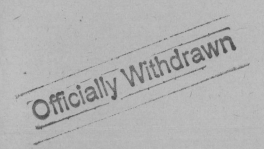

Seeing and Knowing is an eloquent re-affirmation of the aesthetic credo of one of the world's great art critics. At the heart of Bernard Berenson's criticism lies his conviction that the visual art of Western civilization is based on a convention—as much of a convention as the alphabet or mathematical notation—skilfully employed by painters and sculptors to express an idea of order in the chaos of the physical universe.

Illustrating his thesis with reproductions of 88 works of art ranging from cave paintings to Picasso, Berenson contends that the convention of Western art is founded on the artist's acceptance of a compromise between what his eye sees and what his mind knows. He argues that art based on " knowing " alone (so-called " abstract " art) is not worthy of the name of art at all, but merely a jumble of unrecognizable shapes. Likewise, art which attempts to show only what is recorded by the uninformed and unselective eye, is equally confusing. The compromise between the two chaotic extremes of " seeing " and " knowing " Berenson defines as " representation " ; and representational art he believes to be the indispensable base of all visual expression.

Bernard Berenson's primary concern is with the survival of the conventions that grew up during the two great periods of art : the Greco-Roman classical tradition and the Italian Renaissance, particularly with regard to the human form. In the art of the modern period Berenson sees these conventions being relaxed or disregarded. As a result, *Seeing and Knowing* contains a bitter and savage attack on non-representational art, and a memorable excoriation of " modern " painting and sculpture.

Seeing and Knowing is a controversial work. Even those who categorically reject Berenson's verdict against " abstract " art and modern art in general, will appreciate his startling insights and the brilliancy and wit of his prose.

Every book by Bernard Berenson demands the attention of anyone interested in the condition of the visual arts. *Seeing and Knowing* is unquestionably one of the most arresting and provocative of the works of his later years.

NOWING

BERNARD BERENSON

SEEING
AND KNOWING

THE MACMILLAN COMPANY
NEW YORK

FIRST PUBLISHED IN THE UNITED STATES OF AMERICA 1953

PRINTED IN GREAT BRITAIN

TO THE MEMORY OF

BELLE GREENE

SOUL OF

THE MORGAN LIBRARY

ACKNOWLEDGEMENTS

ALINARI : 6, 10, 18, 20, 26, 27, 30, 31, 32, 36, 41, 48, 65

ANDERSON : 34, 45, 51, 56, 57, 58, 59, 62, 63, 66, 67, 70, 76, 79

ANNAN PHOTOGRAPHER, GLASGOW : 82, 83

ARCHAEOLOGISCHES INSTITUT, ROMA : 16, 23

BRAUN : 29

BRITISH MUSEUM : 11, 19, 22

BROGI : 44, 54

CLEVELAND MUSEUM OF ART : 86

DANESI, ROMA : 33

DIRECTION DER BAYER. STAATSGEMÄLDESAMMLUNGEN : 43

FOGG ART MUSEUM, HARVARD UNIVERSITY : 8, 15, 71

FOTO FIORENTINI : 68

FOTOTECA BERENSON : 1, 4, 5a, 5b, 7, 9, 12, 13, 14, 17, 24,
      28, 35, 40, 42, 46, 47, 50a, 50b, 55, 60, 64, 78, 87, 88

GARDNER MUSEUM, BOSTON : 69, 72

LÖWY J. : 52

MORTIMER OFFNER : 49

MUSEO CIVICO, TORINO : 38, 39

MUSEO DI PALEONTOLOGIA, FIRENZE : 2, 3

MUSEUM OF FINE ARTS, BOSTON : 25, 85

NATIONAL GALLERY, LONDON : 74, 75, 80, 81

NATIONAL GALLERY, WASHINGTON : 53

PHOTOGRAPHISCHE GESELLSCHAFT, BERLIN : 61

PHOTO GUSTAV SCHWARZ : 77

from RICHTER : 21

SOPRAINTENDENZA ALLE GALLERIE, FIRENZE : 37, 73

THE ARTS COUNCIL OF GREAT BRITAIN : 84

I

I had been sitting through the first part of the Sienese *Palio*. Not being German, I dispose of a limited quantity of *Sitzfleisch*—flesh to sit with—and was coming to an end. At last, at last the flag-waving (but O how long it did last!) was over, and the flashing by of the galloping horses would only take a moment more.

I do not enjoy unanimity. I suffer from crowd emotion, and resent it. So I had not been too happy under the impact of communal enthusiasm. Besides, I dislike pageants. They are as much a fake as forged pictures, and the descendants of ancient houses who dress up as their forbears have little in common with them except clothes.

So all in all I was glad that the performance had almost reached its end and that soon I would be able to steal away and digest and meditate.

The sun had just set and the afterglow flushed from the red palaces that guard the

theatre-shaped *Piazza* of Siena. I was watching
the flicker of fading light when suddenly I became
aware first of a creeping, then of a crowding, and
finally as of a stream pouring into the paved
arena until it was brim-full or (to change the
simile) jammed tight. With what? If I had
trusted my eyes I should have said with flowers
from a herbaceous border, so multicoloured was
what I actually saw, and I saw nothing else.

In an instant I inferred that the mass, the
crazy-quilt I was looking at, did not consist of
flowers or patchwork. I knew, although in the
growing dimness I could not distinguish heads
or faces, and the jam was such that I saw no
bodies, yet I knew that this floral canopy not
only must be, but was actually, composed of
human beings.

So in Venice from a window on the Grand
Canal, where it opens toward the lagoon, I was
looking diagonally across to San Giorgio. Steam-
boats and motor-launches were going up and
down and were so big in shape and so clearly
articulated, that even at a certain distance I
recognized what they were. But what was it
that packed them tight? Again, as at Siena,
spots of colour suggesting flower gardens rather
than what I unquestioningly assumed they were,

namely passengers. I knew what they must be from experience, not from what was presented to my view. At the same time I kept seeing zig-zaggy criss-cross silhouettes and my eyes alone could not have told me that they were gondoliers standing and rowing in their gondolas.

From my own house between Maiano and Settignano I look over fields to the Arno and to other fields beyond and beyond, rising to meet the graceful dip of the skyline. This receding space is studded pell-mell with rectangular white spots. That is all they are to the eye. I happen to know what the eye does not tell me, that they are houses which the intervening distance prevents me from recognizing for what they are. Much nearer at hand, not many furlongs away, I see masses of green, opaque or translucent or glistening. They are spiky or smooth and, as if supporting them, roughly cylindrical somethings, vaguely brownish, green-ish, greyish. I have learnt in babyhood that they are trees and I vest them with trunks, with branches, with twigs, with foliage, with single leaves, according to their presumed species, ilex, chestnut, pine, olive, although my eyes see only varying shades of green.

Perhaps I am uneasy over this contradiction

between looking and knowing, distressed over having to interpret everything we see beyond, as tangible objects in a familiar space. So I revel in the pictures of a van Eyck (Plate 41) or a Roger van der Weyden (Plate 42), or their so-candid follower, the Master of the Munich panels representing the Life of the Virgin (Plate 43), because they make me traverse space with no fatigue. They attain this object by the exquisitely naïve device of diminishing, as the distance from the eye increases, the size of houses, trees and human figures.

(I for one, along with millions of others who may not think of these matters, am satisfied with their perspective ; yet so far as I know they have not, like Paolo Uccello, kept their wives awake with their tossings over mathematical convergences.)

The fallacy or rather the trick is to make objects, and in particular human figures, no matter how diminished in size, as tangibly visible as if you could touch them. To identify them so clearly and with such detail as they increasingly recede from the eye gives one the feeling that at last one has got into the right kind of world, where sight is not dimmed by distance—truly a life-enhancing experience.

The ensuing paradox arises from the fact that this life-enhancing sense of overcoming spatial distance (while we neither move nor toil) is produced by our being made to see figures as if we had come up with them close at hand ; while—as a matter of fact—at the distance assumed we could not discern the shape with the naked eye except as a vague blur.

We remain unaware of the absurdity because from earliest infancy we have been unconsciously learning to store our minds with generic shapes with which we clothe objects animate and in-animate. When we are given the cue that there is a man somewhere, anywhere, no matter how far away, we think of him as being recognizable, and as having the shape a human male must have. All we admit is that with gradual reces-sion from the angle of vision this creature will diminish in size.

So we are not taken aback, not even surprised, that in most paintings human and, naturally, other animal figures retain their perfectly recog-nizable, tangible shapes at distances where actually they should look like mere blots.

Oddly enough, although Pompeian painting seldom penetrates beyond a middle distance, it blurs shapes at that distance (Plate 31), while a

Degas at a like distance (Plate 85) paints horses and men with shapes, if not features, unchanged.

To reproduce precisely, exactly what appears to the uninformed, untutored, to the so-vaunted " innocent eye " should be, we may assume, the one aim of " impressionist " artists. We should confine the epithet " impressionist " and all its derivatives to representations of purely retinal impressions.

Instead, the epithet is misused in various ways.

The inventors of the term did not apply it to a new and peculiar way of seeing shapes but to the most effective use of pigments for reproducing colour, value and tone as usually seen. If there was novelty it was in their subject-matter, in their preference for the socially unconventional aspects of life, of the workaday, vulgar, even brutal, even repulsive sides of the human lot.

The term was quickly wrenched out of its original use and misunderstood by aestheticians as meaning anything dashed off in a frenzy of creation, by archaeologists as works of art weathered, timeworn, blurred and of uncertain outline and relief : and by most art critics (including myself in the days of ignorance) as swift devil-may-care notation, no matter how incompetent, how absurd, so long as it seemed unlaboured and free.

What we generally call " seeing " is a utilitarian convention, built up in the race since it has been human and perhaps when still " higher animal " ; and in us individuals of to-day by all sorts of contacts and conditionings to which we are submitted during the years prior to self-awareness.

Most of these conventions are strictly concerned with the recognition of objects we want to approach or avoid, but some are representational. It is with these last that we have to do now.

Representation is a compromise with chaos whether visual, verbal, or musical. The compromise prolonged becomes a convention. The convention may last for a season, as is the case with fashion, or for thousands of years, as in ancient Egypt and Mesopotamia as well as in China and most other lands, Asian, African, American, before their contact with hellenized Europeans.

The history of an art should be the account of the successive conventions it has suffered up to date. To a singular degree these conventions have tended to a certain similarity the world over. Until not long ago discussion was rife as to whether they spread from one centre or were due to stages of civilization. Thus neolithic art tends to curious resemblances which convinced many that, for instance, the sculptures of Central America were derived from Egypt or *vice versa*, those of the Nile valley from the heirs of Atlantis, namely, the artists of Yucatan, Guatemala, or Mexico. It is easier to assume that, given a similar way of visualizing, given like tools and materials, the results could not be very different. It is probable that Central Americans did not attain an advanced neolithic use of instruments until many centuries after Egypt became acquainted with iron, and even after the same Egypt began to be altered by Hellenic influence. Assuming that one or two scrawls in Mexico can be identified as copies of Asiatic symbols, they could have affected Mayas and Aztecs no more than Hellenistic representation was affected by an Indian ivory dug up not long ago from the ruins of Pompeii.

If art is as much an animal function in primitive man as in the rest of creation, in birds and beasts, insects and creeping things, then there is no reason for assuming that it was diffused from one centre, any more than the family, the clan, the tribe, the use of fire, the contrivance of shelters, and numberless other arrangements and institutions.

If we wish to think in earnest we must keep in mind unfailingly and constantly that art is convention, although not arbitrary. Conventions that outlast the ages are habitual shortcuts to effective communication, whether the end be practical or representational.

The alphabet is a convention. So is all arithmetical notation. So is mathematics, even the highest. Indeed, it may be the most absolute of conventions without validity outside the mind, if indeed validity exists anywhere outside our so-human minds. The words we use, the words of workaday speech, are conventions. Within us a seething cauldron steaming with stenches and suave vapours ; or a Noah's ark crowded with champing, milling, whirling, fluttering beasts and birds, creeping and crawling things, each standing for a something of ourselves, an incipient sensation, an urge, a wisp of thought, a yearning. Outside our so-called selves the treacherously simplified distance with its illusive but shapeless beyond, as alluring as the pot of gold at the foot of the rainbow, after which I recall running eighty years ago. Above a sky ever changing and ambivalent with cloudy symbols of a high

S.K.—B

romance, but also of terror, horror, doom or of chill, damp, domestic discomfort only. Nearer to the eye the multiplicity, the countlessness of everything, the leaves on the trees, the endless variety of things, animate and inanimate, in the field of vision, moving, never staying put. How name them, how describe them, how classify them and, hardest of all, how stabilize them so that we end by agreeing on what sounds, what outlines, will invariably call up the same words, the same images? Only those who never have attempted to paint or to write ignore what agony it is to communicate to others what one wants to represent or to say. And the joy of creative art comes when one is lured to hope that he has found the cypher, the symbol, the generic shape or scrawl, the hieroglyph, the convention, in short, that will do it. The prosaic task is to prove it and fix it with pen and pencil so that to others it will mean almost what it means to ourselves.

> We cannot kindle when we will
> The fire that in the heart resides,
> The spirit bloweth and is still,
> In mystery our soul abides;
> But tasks in hours of insight will'd
> Can be through hours of gloom fulfill'd.
>
> (Matthew Arnold, *Morality*, lines 1–6.)

Our entire being and doing consists of a series of conventions permanent or successive. We take them so much for granted, we are so unaware of them, that we apply the word "conventional" either to those ways of writing and acting that are losing their hold on us, or to the manners and customs of outsiders, foreigners whom in our heart of hearts we believe subjects for anthropological research while we alone are rational.

(As I write (August 1948) I wonder whether half of our present troubles are not due to conventions regarding international behaviour as old as Homer and long since branded as "absurd", "lethal", "malignant" ghosts from whom we cannot shake ourselves free.)

So long then as we want to have, as we need, as we must have, contact with others of our own species, we can have it only through conventions. If we shed any instinctively or throw them over deliberately, either they are replaced before too long or we fall back into private universes, self-immured, *incommunicado*, as we risk being at present.

I admit of innumerable approaches, conventions of any and every sort, not only in our Europe but everywhere else in all times or places.

Provided of course that the object is not distorted or besmirched or even befouled so that it raises displeasure or even disgust. Provided still more that the object can be, for compromise, instantly recognized.

Literature, Anglo-American literature certainly, is now overshadowed by the glossolaly of Gertrude Stein and still more by the polyglot etymological puns and soap-bubbles of James Joyce. I can see what fun both these jokers must have had. What I cannot understand is that almost the entire literary world of England and America, including responsible university professors, take them seriously, write deliriously or solemnly, and always portentously, about them. Indeed, in a recent weekly, supposed to be one of the most authoritative in Great Britain, *Finnegan's Wake* was compared to the deepest Shakespeare.

It is worse in the visual arts. Words drip with sub-meanings. Take a word out of the colour-vat in our own minds where it soaks ; do what you can to wring it clean, to dry it, to harden it, to crystallize it, as the French have done with their language for three whole centuries until the other day : yet some trace of meaning, besides what is intended, sticks. Not so with straight lines and dots, squares and circles, and other geometrical diagrams in no visual contact with actuality and related to each other only in the executant's impenetrable selfhood. Addicts of cross-word puzzles and kindred games have been trained and exercised (as we all are through play) to excel in the deciphering of these enigmatic messages. Here I reassert that communication is made possible by accepted conventions and by these only, and that the history of all expression, of all the arts, and of the visual arts in particular, should be, can be, nothing but an account, and perhaps an attempt to interpret, its successive conventions.

A tradition, a convention, needs constant manipulation to vivify it, to enlarge it, to keep it fresh and supple, and capable of generating problems and producing their solution. To keep a convention alive and growing fruitfully requires creative genius, and when that fails it either becomes mannered and academic or runs " amok ", as in the last few decades. The first happened to Florentine art about 1550, to Venetian art about 1600 (although it had an aftermath in the XVIIIth century), to Flemish art in the XVIth century until it was reinvigorated and renewed by Rubens and Van Dyck.

But from the XIIth to the XXth century somewhere in our world, in our part of Europe, a
genius never failed to come to the rescue, who
seized the convention, vitalized it, and handed
it on.

II

The visual arts—(excepting architecture to the
extent only that it does not depend on appeals
to our sense of weight and support, to our
breathing, to our feelings for space)—the visual
arts are, I repeat, a compromise between what
we see and what we know.

The Palaeolithics of Biscaya and the Dordogne
(Plate 1) had to learn to see how the bison looked
and how he moved so that they might get at him
with spike or javelin or sling. Few representations of animals in action surpass the paintings
of Altamira (Plate 2). In bone scratchings of
the same period deer stalk through reedy
marshes. The last betray a certain awareness of
surroundings, which foreshadows landscape. The

hunted is there, but the hunter, the man, seldom appears, and in the few cases when he does, you would scarcely know him for human. Not being pursued for food, he did not interest the artist.

Indeed it was only in the Aurignacian period that sculptors began to represent the human figure, beginning with females like the so-called Venuses found in South East and South Central Europe (Plate 3). They have breasts like bottles, huge behinds, small almost featureless faces, and are startlingly like the masterpieces of the most admired wood and stone carvers of our own day.

With scant anticipations, as for instance at Kôm-el-Ahmar, Egypt no later than 3000 B.C. offered a completely thought-out convention of the human nude, female as well as male (Plate 4), so satisfactory to the sculptor that it suffered scarcely any change till it collided with the Hellenistic concept ; so standardized that the upper part of a figure could be done by one artist and the lower by another living far away. Knowing had got so much the better of seeing that for more than 2,000 years artist and public understood each other without discussion, accepted their visual limitations and enabled the craftsman to produce in every material those masterpieces of figure art the enjoyment of which is even now so much of paradise.

At this point I beg the reader to have patience if I insert a few words about the differences between Egyptian and Mesopotamian figure arts, and venture to suggest the reason why they differ.

It is possible that objects in wood and other fragile materials, as well as painted surfaces, have perished owing to the marshy land and damp climate of Mesopotamia. Among Meso-potamian figures there are no young girls in their nude loveliness offering lotuses, no subtly deli-cate wood-carvings of youthful females swimming and holding things out of water (Plate 5), no groups in clay or wood of sturdy peasants pound-ing (Plate 8), no robust women kneading and rolling (Plate 6), such as we find so frequently in Egyptian paintings, sculptures and *objets d'art*. Until the Assyrian period Mesopotamian statues and reliefs never show people without clothes, clothes that seldom articulate the bodies they cover and scarcely distinguish between the sexes (Plate 10). The artists seem to have avoided nakedness and never to have felt the desire of exalting the naked to the nude. I cannot recall unclothed figures in the arts of the

Land-between-the-Rivers until Hellenistic influence produced the innumerable figurines of
the fertility goddess. These are, however, more
naked than nude with their projecting hips and
sagging bellies.

This is not the place to compare the achieve-
ments of Nile and Euphrates. They are now dis-
cussed more for priority than quality. The first
question when settled will leave open the other,
namely, that of quality. There the answer seems
clear. Despite a certain muddiness of envelope
and sloppiness of contour, due perhaps to its
having begun with clay as its only material,
Mesopotamian art had much to its credit : as,
for instance, a grave and imposing masculinity in
its statues (Plate 9), and in the Assyrian period,
action of the highest order and the dawn of a
modern feeling for space (Plates 11–13). But
its range was limited. Never playful, never gay,
never elegant, never expressive of joy on the
part of the artist, or of delight on the part of his
public. Let me repeat that this conclusion may
be drawn from the absence of artefacts which
might modify this impression, perhaps, but not
obliterate it.

Minor objects depend even more than monumental ones on mastery of the nude. The fact

that the Mesopotamians have ignored it may be a reason (among others, no doubt, but likely enough the principal one) why their art is so limited in subject-matter and so lacking in delicacy, in refinement, in charm. These qualities can be obtained only when the draughtsman has the same command of the articulations of the human body that the poet has over the vocabulary and idiom he is using. Without it, who could have made the drawings on Greek vases of the early Vth century B.C. (Plates 22, 23), or the figurines known as " Tanagra " (Plate 24) and thousands of other objects from the Nile-Aegean lands, which it is a joy to look at, to caress, to dream over (Plate 7) ? Egypt and Hellas and their daughters Italy and France have surpassed all other peoples in the advantage they have taken of the nude for every conceivable representation, no matter how monumental, how static, how active, how grave, how playful (Plate 25).

The nude is a convention that it took thousands of years to perfect and impose and render so familiar to civilized man that he no longer distinguishes it from " nature ". It would seem that like most of our notions it started out as a concept of generic shape. When a child I drew wasp-like tiny creatures hopping like fleas over the paper. As an adult I discovered that at a certain stage of mental and manual development, similar representations of our species were found scratched on every kind of surface all over the earth—among Sioux and other American Indians of the Great Plains as late as, if not later than, a hundred years ago. This palaeolithic state of mind gave way as under compulsion man learned to observe. In Egypt the urge may have come from the anxiety to produce statues that the Ka could not fail to recognize as himself. In Hellas it seems to have been due to the sheer curiosity of the sublime ape that was the Greek, combined with the itch of his hand to shape and model and refine. He experimented with figures like the Helladic, looking like cellos or a certain kind of bottle with a small middle and a round-knobbed or spiky stopper (Plate 14) ; or with cake-walking busts and bird-like legs as in Minoan art (Plate 15), which continued into the Dipylon of about 1000 B.C. (Plate 16). Then toward 700 B.C., after the discovery of the Nile and its eye-opening wonders, he began to carve figures of young men (and no doubt to draw them as well), which led him through early Athens (Plate 17), through Olympia (Plate 18), through

Argos, through Sikyon to Polyclites, to Phidias (Plate 19), to Praxiteles (Plates 20, 21), to Lysippus and their hosts.

The quest was for a compromise between concept and observation in representing the human figure. Oscillating, vibrating, easily pulled this way and that way, the compromise known as " the nude " has lasted on to our own day except for periods of occultation like our so-called " Dark " and " Middle " Ages. At the end of this last dark period in the North, its greatest artistic genius, Albrecht Dürer, thought of nothing so much as acquiring this canon (Plates 26, 27). It is now suffering another occultation, but this time only partial, and it is hoped of no protracted duration.

III

This partial occultation is due to many causes. Two or three may be selected as reasons for its suddenness, as well as for its feeling so self-important, so self-caressing.

The exhibitions of phases of representational art prior to the Mediterranean classical, excavated by archaeologists or discovered by explorers, and their reproduction in illustrated papers, have tended to unsettle the already *blasé* visual concepts and convictions of painters and sculptors.

Just before the first world war a genius of mercantile propaganda arrived in Paris and settled down on the ground floor of a building close to the Palais Bourbon. There he displayed and showed off Negro wood-carvings of human shapes and ventriloquized about them with phrases that were quickly taken up by the most authoritative art critics in Paris, London and New York.

It would take a Balzac to describe the power and the glory of gifted dealers and their influence for good and for evil over the public. Not easy to overpraise the Durand-Ruels, the Wildensteins, or a Vollard, for what they did to popularize the great " impressionists " from Manet to Cézanne. Less conscientious tradesmen worked through their stooges. I remember one of them boasting that until his recent and so successful invasion of the art market, he had been a corn-broker.

The idolized poets, painters, sculptors and critics after the first world war gave vent to the feeling of despair regarding the future by expressing their contempt for everything in the social order, in politics, and in all the arts that had brought them to that pass.

Ever since about 700 B.C. (when, thanks to the Greeks, art began to be progressive) visual concepts, visual convictions, that is to say visual conventions, have been nibbled at and distorted by the craving for novelty, by the conceit of expecting to do better, or by any other urge to exercise function more freely, more effectively and more advantageously. It happened more or less unconsciously, timidly and always with the hope of perfecting an art, never with the deliberate purpose of throwing over the accumulated treasure of traditions and skills hard won in the course of so many centuries. Even the " Dark Ages ", through a deep and general decline of civilization—for which as yet, even after a second world war, there has been no parallel—went on working, not clearly on the lines of a classical past but certainly not in deliberate opposition to it. It is in our own day that for the first time in history a long-accepted classical tradition with all its invaluable conventions has been wantonly, jeeringly thrown away. The damage done will not be made good by penitential moods of uncertain sincerity and proposals to find salvation by creeping back into the womb of the Mother of All Things.

In the figure arts it has meant throwing away composition, for which already a Degas had shown a distaste that in the long run will count against him. It was accompanied by the conclusion not based on seeing, on observing, but on exasperation and on the preconceived assumption that the squalid, the sordid, the violent, the bestial, the misshapen, in short that low life was the only " reality ".

Painters turned for their inspiration not to the great masters of all centuries but to those, whether competent or incompetent, whose subject-matter fanned their fury against the Greeks. So they studied Goya, Daumier, Lautrec and Forain and, in the more distant past, the inflated and brutal vulgarities of Caravaggio's crudest followers, and further back the daubers of the XIth and XIIth centuries (Plate 35), touchingly expressive but as ignorant and incompetent as painters of recent years have aspired to be.

Every misuse of the human figure was preached, pictured and praised. Nothing was dreaded so much as being academic, that is to say, having a standardized concept, a convention with regard to the nude. The most remarkable draughts-man still alive has taken every advantage of his skill to hide his true gifts (Plates 28, 29). Perhaps in deepest secret he draws in orthodox fashion everything he bedevils while painting, as I have been assured Joyce wrote out in plain King's English what he fricasséed for his printed prose. Likewise the one painter in " Zentral-Europa " who composes and paints and illustrates in a way to survive the tossings and nauseas of seasonal fashions, feels obliged to obscure his purpose with puerile malpractices. Anything to get away from the sane-asylum which for thousands of years art has been trying to erect in the mad-house welter of chaos.

These routes might have stumbled on a path that leads back to sobriety and sanity ; for withal they had not utterly abandoned the world of concrete, tangible, let us say " objective ", things of lived actuality. A remotely parallel move-ment at the end of the Gothic period, with its spidery architecture, recklessly calligraphic draperies, and affected smiles, ended not in a blind alley but in a reaction that produced the van Eycks and Rogier and Conrad Witz and Fouquet and Masaccio and Brunelleschi and Bramante.

As yet, however, no reaction against the chopping and juggling, distorting and fooling with shapes ! No leader, no guide has appeared. When a small boy of seven or eight, at an age when for fear of being laughed at one dare not ask questions, I gave up trying to draw a table, because I despaired of showing the underside as well as the upper one. *On a changé tout cela.* Nowadays it is only what cannot be represented visibly that interests the " artist " of the day. Visceral, intestinal and meaningless cerebral activities, with no conceivable visual shape, or even concept of a shape, but known to exist, absorb the limner to the severe exclusion of the sensible, sensuous, sensual world of the eye. And thus " knowing " is now revelling in a victory, a " knock-out "—a short one, let us hope —over " seeing ". Worse still : in despair of finding a way back to art, to what is now called " representational art "—as if there could be visual art that is not representational or based on what has been represented—in cowardly despair, painters and sculptors, painters more particularly, have deserted the world of concrete shapes with all that the craftsman seeing and conventionalizing could make of them, and have taken to geometrizing, to abstracting, to " non-representational art ".

The term " abstract art ", like such contradictions in terms as a wet dryness, an icy heat, or a soft hardness, may be conceivable to the mind but scarcely to the senses. For many thousands of years visual art has been based on ideated sensations, on a compromise between what one knows and what one sees and between what one sees and what one can reproduce for others. It therefore would seem to correspond to a continuous need or desire or demand of human nature, of man who is matter and spirit, body as well as mind. It is not likely that he will be henceforth satisfied with the store of geometrical squares, lozenges, diagonals, circles, globes, trapezoids, parallelepipedons when he asks for the bread of art. No perfection in smearing canvas or wood or paper with faint colours, guaranteed to represent nothing, no skill in buttering surfaces with pigments, as a good and faithful nursemaid or Werther's Charlotte buttered bread, will replace pictures ; no segments of globes in wood or stone, no matter how caressingly polished and put together so as to suggest broad-bottomed, deep-breasted females, will replace multimillennial sculpture.

Neolithic artists had their reasons for doing women with colossal buttocks and huge breasts. They were interested only in the reproductive functions of the females and reproduced these only with scarcely a thought of face and features. Have sculptors and painters of to-day the same magical purpose ?

What enjoyment this kind of designing procures with chalks, inks, paint, and even clay, marble, bronze, is not seriously aesthetic but frivolously intellectualistic, like cross-word puzzles and similar caricatures of noble games like chess.

If by " abstract art " is meant geometrical shapes as distinct from those the average man thinks he sees in what he calls " nature ", then surely that art exists nowadays in great abundance and with fascinating elegance of its own in our machinery and in what this machinery turns out.

From the elegant instruments of destruction to well-shaped vehicles, from the intricate devices for precision to toys and writing-table gadgets and delicate toilet articles, I suck delight from shapes that enjoy the exquisite economy of the perfect adaptation of means to ends. And that is a beauty in its own way, as the beauty of genre or, on another level, the beauty of Holiness.

If that be so, why try to juggle with disembodied lines and curves that can have none but a strictly incapsulated private meaning ?

So there is but one way out of the brambly maze in which we are blindly beating about : follow the tenuous beam of reason that will lead us back to the compromise between " seeing " and " knowing ", between retinal vision and conceptual looking, on which rests visual art as an eternal function of human nature. Purely conceptual patterns, if seriously pursued, can end in pure mathematics only. An eminent pioneer of that sublime pursuit assured me that its practice gave him visions and ecstasies beyond belief. Unfortunately the highest mathematics is beyond the understanding of those who have not learned its language, a language given to few to master. With little effort, and some training, visual art is communicable and intelligible universally.

IV

Let us go back to the earlier part of this talk which had a beginning, has no middle and will have no end, because there is no conceivable finality to what one may say about things not quantitative—and even then! (Statistics are quantitative, but what easier than to manipulate them with every evil intention!)

I ventured to say that our compromise of the human figure, our canon of it, will outlast the rebellion now raging against it. Dadaists, Surrealists, etc., have done nothing but exploit it and then have shirked the struggle and deserted from life and living things and men and women and nature for a Nirvana of abstraction. This compromise, this canon of the human figure, has been studied in a delightfully humanistic book by the Dane Conrad Lange and in a most detailed and learned work by the Italian Alessandro Della Seta, and need not be pursued further here.

Let us hope that students as gifted and as

learned will hasten to give us what, so far as I
know, is still lacking, an equally illuminating
treatise on the compromise which, next to that
of the human figure, plays the most important
part in representational art—I refer to landscape.[1]

I have already touched upon its humble be-
ginnings in the Aurignacian or Magdalenian age
and its modest progress until the Hellenistic
period.   In the surviving wall paintings as well
as in the so-called Alexandrian reliefs (Plates
30, 31) we find representations of the out-of-doors
that are idyllically suburban with scarcely a
background ;   foliage treated conceptually and
trees, generally stone-pines, often wind-tossed
(Plate 32), as in nature they are apt to be when
near the sea.

From this to the landscape convention perfected by Giorgione and Titian and their
followers and successors down to the other day,
would have been but a step if Antique art had
continued to discover better and ever better
conventions for representing microcosm and
macrocosm.   Instead, it declined to the require-

---

[1] Since writing this, K. Clark's book, *Landscape into Art*,
has appeared, anticipated to some extent by Max Fried-
länder's on the same subject.   A forgotten book published
by Murray in 1885 also deserves mention : Josiah Gilbert's
Landscape in Art before Claude and Salvatore.

ments of a slum society. The human figure could not be entirely ignored even in the catacombs (Plate 34), where it had an indispensable rôle as a crude didactic hieroglyph—shall we say as " *art engagé* ". But the outer world ceased to interest a civilization, a society reduced to hiding in hovels, cellars and make-shift shelters piled up out of the crumbs of past amenities.

Art survived after a fashion at Constantinople and its coasts and with the Macedonian emperors continued by the Comneni settled on a formula for landscape that we find in the Menologia (Plate 33) and other illustrated manuscripts as well as in mosaics. It was reduced to escarped, ribbed hills with an opening like an inverted triangle in the middle, and one or two trees growing out of the metallic rock. These trees as a rule consisted of a thin stem and a thick tuft. A relatively naturalistic painting of a plant or two appeared in the crinkled fore-edge.

This token landscape which satisfied the mediaeval world gave place without rhyme or reason, with no notice of impending change, to exquisite evocations of dewy distances and cool space that we can still enjoy in the Trivulzio *Book of Hours* (Plates 38, 39)—but no longer in the Turin one, destroyed by fire some decades ago (Plate 40). If not by the van Eycks, then by an artist as inventive and creative. With them (Plate 41), and their followers in the Low Countries, began and prospered and triumphed the views, the scenery that reached their culmination in Patinier and Henri de Bles (Plates 44, 45), and declined for a hundred years or more, to be reinvigorated, restated by Rubens, a Fleming who, as no other northerner, profited by the sunlight and the bread and wine of Italy.

Rubens (Plate 70) brought Titian to the North, the Titian who perfected the concept of landscape (Plate 68) and gave it generic shapes which, with all sorts of variants, prevailed well into the XIXth century.

This receipt massed lush foliage in graceful assemblage with crisp edges, and revelled in glen-like middle distances and romantic horizons. Colour glowing and radiant, tending to rich brown. This pattern of " nature ", in which both seeing and knowing united to create the scenery best suited to a sensuously idyllic yet noble existence, had become by the beginning of the XIXth century so juiceless, so shrivelled that little was left except the brown tree.

I cannot recall in what English author, whether Northcote or Haydon or Leslie, I read of a discussion about the way they were painting trees. One of the interlocutors was challenging the other to look out of the window and discover one as brown as they were doing them.

The Titianesque landscape was succeeded by the experimental one furthered by Constable (Plates 80, 81) and pursued by many zestful painters of the last century, French for the most part, culminating in Cézanne (Plate 88). My admiration for their effort is boundless, and could Cézanne have been succeeded by talents like his own, who knows but that landscape might now be well on the way to translating into his, Cézanne's, terms the space compositions of Perugino (Plate 51) and Raphael (Plate 52), the idylls of Giorgione (Plates 65, 66) and Titian (Plates 67–69), the grave magnificence of Poussin (Plates 76, 77) and the enchantments of Claude Lorrain (Plate 78) and Turner (Plate 86). But it ended with a bump !

A convention is largely a matter of notation as, to an overwhelming degree, are mere fashions. In the painting of landscape foliage is a most important element. How to convey a sense of its incalculable detail requires an unusually careful compromise between seeing and knowing. Except when close at hand we see masses of green with dabs of yellow and russet, or sparkling amber and crimson leafage and spiky outlines. Ribbed and ragged conifers represented trees in Mesopotamian art (Plates 11–13), and reference has already been made to the way they were conventionalized in ripe and late Antiquity as well as in the Middle Ages. Thus in Byzantine mosaics (now for the most part found on Italian soil only) (Plates 36, 37) trees could take the highly conventionalized shape of elaborate patterns as remote from what we call " nature " as the foliage in XVIth-century Persian rugs.

The revival of curiosity in the XVth century led to the observation that foliage was composed of single leaves and accordingly the temptation to paint each leaf, as even in a Perugino or Raphael, must have been hard to overcome, and seldom was before Giorgione and Titian. No notation more successful than the compromise of the two last between seeing and knowing, sight and concept. No wonder their convention lasted till the other day.

Early in that century, before Giorgione and Titian, Fra Angelico treated distances in a startlingly unconceptual way (Plate 46). With a medium as ductile, as plastic, as Cézanne exploited, the one beatified artist might have anticipated that master to an interesting degree.

Angelico's younger contemporary, Filippo Lippi, painted forest glens with a freshness evocative of mushrooms and other earthy and herby odours (Plate 47). Neither was taken up because with Baldovinetti (Plate 48) and with the Pollajuolo (Plate 49) the topographic, almost cartographic, interest based on mathematical perspective prevailed, and no doubt the absorbing preoccupation with the nude militated against intensive interest in the outer world. For which reason Michelangelo's reluctant landscapes are as abstract as those of the aged Degas in his pastels. Botticelli offers but glimpses through windows, and then of flowers and foliage chiefly. Except in his Berlin Saint Sebastian (Plate 50) and to some degree in his frescoes of the Sistine Chapel, I can recall no extensive views of the out-of-doors. As for Leonardo, although himself a magician in the art of transfiguring nature, he had little but contempt for landscape, Botticelli's in particular, and wrote that all you had to do to paint one was to slap any clear surface with a sponge dipped in pigment. Or was it a malicious hint that such a result was truer to actual seeing than the over-conceptual one then obtained and obtaining ? Later Florentine landscape, I mean that of Piero di Cosimo,

Fra Bartolommeo (Plate 53), Andrea del Sarto, Franciabigio, etc., did not go much beyond Perugino's patterns, although Fra Bartolommeo and Andrea felt the influence of Giorgione, while Piero di Cosimo (Plate 54) in his later years suffered the attraction of German engravings.

North Italian Quattrocento painting was over-shadowed by Mantegna (Plate 55), who circum-scribed man and " nature ", and all the shapes he saw, with the precise and elegant contours he willed them to have. The effect is of being transported to a gem-like, jewel-like world, as man-made and owing as little to nature as Venice does as a town. His Ferrarese followers, Tura, Cossa, Ercole Roberti (Plates 56–58), go even further in creating worlds of hard semi-precious stones, strange edifices and fabulous distances. But two of Mantegna's followers, Girolamo da Cremona (Plate 60) and Liberale da Verona (Plate 59), discovered in their minia-tures the fascination of the dawn, and his brother-in-law Giovanni Bellini the sky after sun-rise and before sunset (Plates 61–63), as well as settled serene full daylight. Bellini's presenta-tions of nature, although over-conceptual from our point of view and held back by knowing from seeing and therefore given to an over-naïve notation (compare his foliage with Titian's in the Feast of the Gods (Plate 64), where both painted successively), are yet, throughout his long career, among the most impressive and most transporting in existence. He was, if not the inventor, one of the earliest painters of the emotional and even the Romantic landscape— the landscape which with all sorts of develop- ments and variations led through Giorgione (Plates 65–66) and Titian (Plates 67–69), Rubens (Plate 70) and Salvator Rosa (Plate 71), Both (Plate 74) and Cuyp (Plate 75), Rem- brandt (Plate 72) and Seghers (Plate 73), Claude (Plate 78) and the Vernets (Plate 79), the Norwich School (Plates 80–82) and Turner (Plate 86), to Corot (Plates 83, 84), and to the so-called " impressionists ", almost to our own day (Plates 85, 87, 88).

V

I have done, but not ended. There is no end to what one can hope to discover and think about any subject of interest. Every serious subject is infinite.

I do not want the reader to leave me with the idea that I expect the confusion, struttings, blusterings, solemn puerilities that are now practised, taught, admired and proclaimed to last for ever. The man-quake through which we have been reeling during the last fifty years may trouble us for another fifty years, another hundred years ; yet what is even a century in the history of mankind ! We have been through as much again and again in the last few thousand years. We shall settle down some day and stop enjoying the sadistic or masochistic pleasure of ignoring or combating all values except those that arise from the part of us that is below the belt. Eyes and ears will reconquer their rights to inform head and heart, and these will use them for new compromises between seeing and knowing, between feeling and thinking.

In the past ages, art has sunk as low, although probably with no such smirking self-adulation, as it has to-day. After the collapse of Aegean civilization somewhere around 1500 B.C., there followed a decline, a desiccation known as the Geometrical style. It reduced the human figure to isosceles triangles meeting at their apexes

(Plate 16), which served as waistline. It had many affinities with the abstract art of to-day and would have equalled it, had not artists arisen with the will, the gift and steadfastness to work zestfully until they attained the compromise between seeing and knowing that we call " Greek art ".

After the internal and external disasters that overtook the Roman Empire, representational art sank so low, in the Latin part of it at least, that sculpture almost entirely disappeared and painting produced but vague and involuntarily grotesque attempts to reproduce human shapes. Where Byzantine influences could persist, as in Italy, in Catalonia, in Ottonian Germany, the disintegration was never complete and recovery began earlier. In inaccessible regions like the French Massif Central we can still descry frescoes of the XIth and even XIIth centuries (Plate 35) which illustrate Holy Writ and Golden Legend with figures and compositions of a crudity and absurdity that rouse the admiration of critics and perhaps the envy of certain painters of to-day. Yet by 1300 Italy had its Cavallini, its Cimabue, its Giotto as well as the Pisani, and France and Germany already had Moissac and Saint Gilles, Chartres, Rheims and Amiens, Bamberg, Naumburg and Meissen.

Representational art is a function of anthropoids ever since they have been human, and it may be doubted whether illustrated papers and the movies will put a stop to the psycho-physiological urge to create with a more subtle instrument than the camera.

I do not hesitate to prophesy a revival of sculpture and painting as arts based on the human nude as the essential, the vital factor in figure representation. We shall come to a new compromise between seeing and knowing which will serve as a rolling platform for the artists whom it will carry on to new visions and new creations.

VALLOMBROSA,
    SUMMER 1948.

LIST OF PLATES

S.K.—D

11 Transport of a colossal statue of a winged bull in the high valley of the Tigris. Bas-relief in alabaster from the Palace of Sennacherib (705/681 B.C.) at Nineveh. (*British Museum, London.*)

12 Archers of Ashurbanapal (668/626 B.C.). Bas-relief in alabaster from Nineveh. (*Louvre, Paris.*)

13 Cattle and Prisoners of Ashurbanapal (669/626 B.C.). Bas-relief in alabaster from Nineveh. (*Louvre, Paris.*)

14 Helladic Idols (Bronze Age). (*National Museum, Athens.*)

15 Cretan painted relief at Knossos (reproduction). (*Fogg Art Museum, Cambridge, Mass.*)

16 Funerary Bowl from Dipylon (VIIIth century B.C.). (*National Museum, Athens.*)

17 Kouros (end of the VIIth century B.C.). (*Metropolitan Museum, New York.*)

18 Heracles, Athena and the Stymphalian Birds. Metope from Olympia (first decades of the Vth century B.C.). (*Louvre, Paris.*)

19 Centaur and Lapith. Metope from the Parthenon (Vth century B.C.). (*British Museum, London.*)

20 Young Athlete resting. Copy from Praxiteles the Elder (480/420 B.C.). (*Barracco Museum, Rome.*)

21 The Venus of Cnidos, after Praxiteles (recon-
    structed copy). (*From Richter : " The Sculpture
    of the Greeks* ".)

22 Douris (first decades of the Vth century B.C.).
    Red-figured psykter with satyrs. (*British
    Museum, London.*)

23 Women at Toilet. Red-figured vase (Vth century
    B.C.). (*Glyptothek, Munich.*)

24 Two Women gossiping. Greek terra-cotta (IIIrd
    century B.C.). (*British Museum, London.*)

25 Germain Pilon (?) : Fountain. (*Museum of Fine
    Arts, Boston.*)

26 Albrecht Dürer : Adam. (*Pitti Palace, Florence.*)

27 Albrecht Dürer : Eve. (*Pitti Palace, Florence.*)

28 Pablo Picasso : Portrait of Vollard (drawing).
    (*Metropolitan Museum, New York.*)

29 Pablo Picasso : Woman 1938. (*Private Collec-
    tion.*)

30 Polyphemos. Hellenistic bas-relief. (*Villa Albani,
    Rome.*)

31 The Rape of Europa. Pompeian fresco. (*Na-
    tional Museum, Naples.*)

32 Ulysses and the Laestrygones. (*Fresco, Vatican,
    Rome.*)

43 Master of the Life of the Virgin : The Visitation with a Donor (detail). (*Alte Pinacothek, Munich.*)

44 Henri Met de Bles : The Coppermine. (*Uffizi, Florence.*)

45 Joachim Patinier : Saint Jerome. (*Prado, Madrid.*)

46 Fra Angelico : Deposition (detail). (*San Marco Museum, Florence.*)

47 Fra Filippo : Nativity (detail). (*Kaiser Friedrich Museum, Berlin.*)

48 Baldovinetti : Nativity (detail). Fresco in the cloisters of SS. Annunziata, Florence.

49 Antonio Pollajuolo : The Rape of Dejanira (detail). (*Jarves Collection, New Haven.*)

50 Botticelli : Saint Sebastian (detail). (*Kaiser Friedrich Museum, Berlin.*)

51 Perugino : Crucifixion. Fresco in S. Maria Maddalena de' Pazzi, Florence.

52 Raphael : Madonna. (*Gallery, Dresden.*)

53 Fra Bartolommeo : The Creation of Eve. (*National Gallery of Art, Washington.*)

54 Piero di Cosimo : Perseus and Andromeda (detail). (*Uffizi, Florence.*)

55 Mantegna : Saint Jerome. (*Museum, São Paolo, Brazil.*)

56 Ercole Roberti : The Argonauts. (*Picture Gallery, Padua.*)

57 Francesco Del Cossa : Legend of Saint Hyacinth (detail). (*Vatican Gallery, Rome.*)

58 Cosmè Tura : Saint Jerome in the Wilderness. (*National Gallery of Art, London.*)

59 Liberale de Verona : Adoration of the Magi. (*Cathedral, Verona.*)

60 Girolamo da Cremona : Miniature (Gr. N/8). (*Cathedral Library, Siena.*)

61 Giovanni Bellini : Resurrection. (*Kaiser Friedrich Museum, Berlin.*)

62 Giovanni Bellini : Madonna in Landscape. (*National Gallery of Art, London.*)

63 Giovanni Bellini : Allegory. (*Uffizi, Florence.*)

64 Giovanni Bellini (and Titian) : The Feast of the Gods. (*National Gallery of Art, Washington.*)

65 Giorgione : " Fête champêtre ". (*Louvre, Paris.*)

66 Giorgione : The Tempest. (*Academy, Venice.*)

67 Titian : " Noli me tangere ". (*National Gallery of Art, London.*)

68 Titian : The Venus of the Pardo (detail). (*Louvre, Paris.*)

69 Titian : The Rape of Europa. (*Gardner Museum, Boston.*)

70 Rubens : Landscape with Harvesters. (*Pitti Palace, Florence.*)

71 Salvator Rosa : Landscape. (*Fogg Art Museum, Cambridge, Mass.*)

72 Rembrandt : Landscape with Obelisk. (*Gardner Museum, Boston.*)

73 Hercules Seghers : Landscape. (*Uffizi, Florence.*)

74 Jan Both : Landscape. (*National Gallery of Art, London.*)

75 Aelbert Cuyp : Cattle and Horses. (*National Gallery of Art, London.*)

76 Nicolas Poussin : Diogenes throws away his Drinking-bowl. (*Louvre, Paris.*)

77 Nicolas Poussin : St. John at Patmos. (*Kaiser Friedrich Museum, Berlin.*)

78 Claude Lorrain : Carlo and Ubaldo embarking in pursuit of Rinaldo. (*Thiessen Collection, Lugano.*)

79 Claude J. Vernet : Bathers. (*Louvre, Paris.*)

80 J. Constable : The Hay-wain. (*National Gallery of Art, London.*)

81 J. Constable : Weymouth Bay. (*National Gallery of Art, London.*)

82 J. S. Cotman : Castle Eden Dean. (*National Gallery of Scotland, Edinburgh.*)

83 J. B. C. Corot : The Goat-herd. (*National Gallery of Scotland, Edinburgh.*)

84 J. B. C. Corot : View of the Château de Pierre-fonds. (*Musée, Quimper.*)

85 H. G. E. Degas : Carriages at Races. (*Museum of Fine Arts, Boston.*)

86 J. M. W. Turner : Sunset. (*Museum of Fine Arts, Cleveland.*)

87 A. Renoir : Landscape. (*Metropolitan Museum, New York.*)

88 Cézanne : Mont St. Victoire and Viaduct. (*Private Collection.*)

BISON. CAVE PAINTING AT ALTAMIRA. REPRODUCED BY ABBÉ BREUIL.

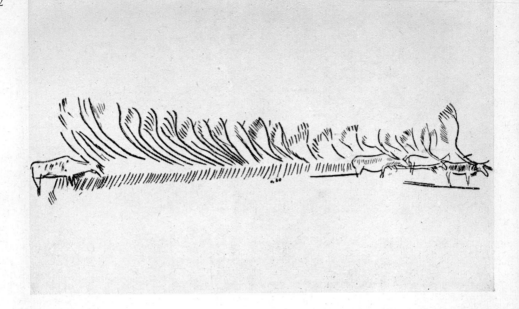

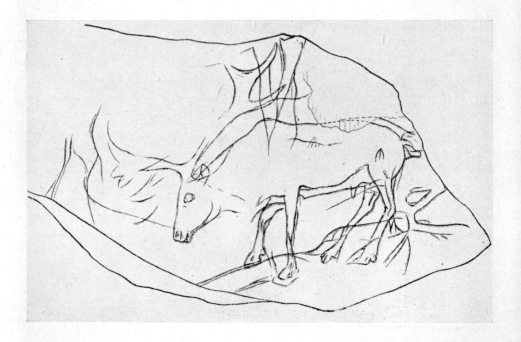

MAGDALENIAN SCRATCHINGS ON BONE AND STONE.

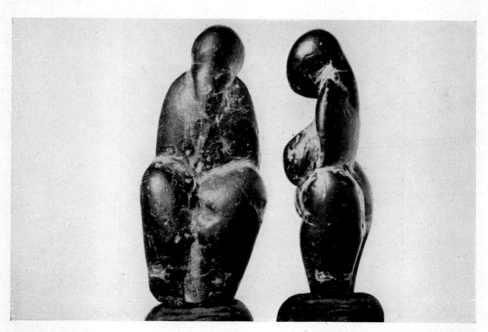

THREE AURIGNACIAN « VENUSES » (FROM WILLENDORF, SAVIGNANO, MENTONE).

4

STATUE OF PRINCE HEM-ON (CIRCA 2900 B. C.). PELIZAEUS MUSEUM, HILDESHEIM.

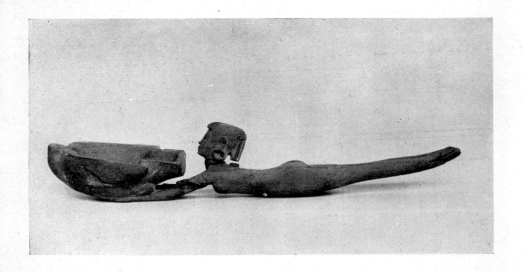

TWO SPOONS FOR FACE-PAINT (CIRCA 1500 B. C.). LOUVRE, PARIS AND BRITISH MUSEUM, LONDON.

WOMAN GRINDING GRAIN (CIRCA 2000 B. C.). ARCHAEOLOGICAL MUSEUM, FLORENCE.

FEMALE DANCER. LIMESTONE FRAGMENT (CIRCA 1500 B. C.). EGYPTIAN MUSEUM, TURIN.

8

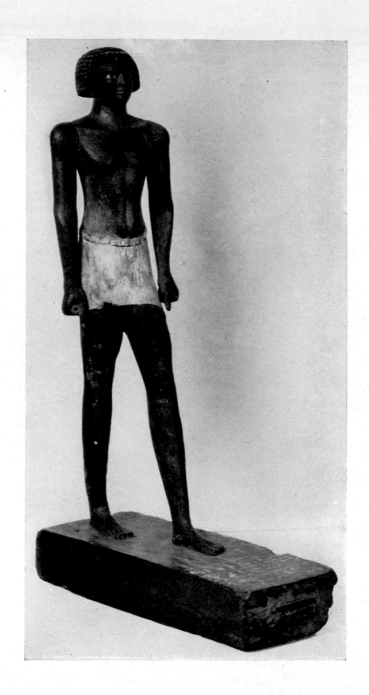

WOODEN STATUETTE OF A SLAVE (CIRCA 2400 B. C.). FOGG ART MUSEUM, CAMBRIDGE (MASS.).

PORTRAIT OF PRINCE GUDEA (CIRCA 2400 B. C.). STOCLET COLLECTION, BRUXELLES.

ATTENDANTS OF SARGON II (722/705 B. C.). BASRELIEF FROM KHORSABAD. LOUVRE, PARIS.

TRANSPORT OF A COLOSSAL STATUE OF A WINGED BULL IN THE HIGH VALLEY OF THE TIGRIS. BASRELIEF IN ALABASTER FROM THE PALACE OF SENNACHERIB (705/681 B. C.) AT NINEVEH. BRITISH MUSEUM, LONDON.

ARCHERS OF ASHURBANAPAL (669/626 B. C.). BASRELIEF IN ALABASTER FROM NINEVEH. LOUVRE, PARIS.

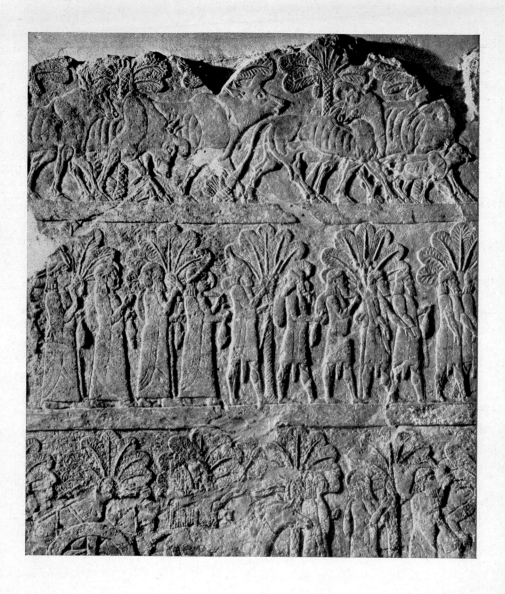

CATTLE AND PRISONERS OF ASHURBANAPAL (669/626 B. C.). BASRELIEF IN ALABASTER FROM NINEVEH. LOUVRE, PARIS.

HELLADIC IDOLS (BRONZE AGE). NATIONAL MUSEUM, ATHENS.

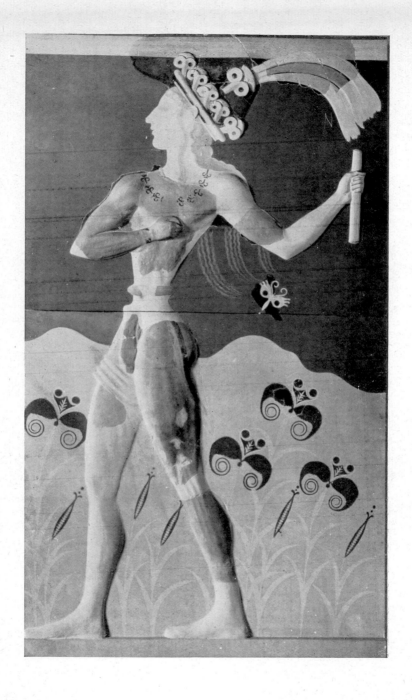

CRETAN PAINTED RELIEF AT KNOSSOS (COPY). FOGG ART MUSEUM, CAMBRIDGE (MASS.).

FUNERARY BOWL FROM DIPYLON (8TH CENTURY B. C.). NATIONAL MUSEUM, ATHENS.

KOUROS (END OF 7TH CENTURY B. C.). METROPOLITAN MUSEUM, NEW YORK.

HERACLES, ATHENA AND THE STYMPHALIAN BIRDS. METOPE FROM OLYMPIA (FIRST DECADES OF
THE 5TH CENTURY B. C.). LOUVRE, PARIS.

CENTAUR AND LAPITH. METOPE FROM THE PARTHENON (5TH CENTURY B. C.). BRITISH MUSEUM, LONDON.

YOUNG ATHLETE RESTING. COPY AFTER PRAXITELES THE ELDER (480/420 B. C.). BARRACCO MUSEUM, ROME.

THE VENUS OF CNIDOS AFTER PRAXITELES (RECONSTRUCTED COPY). FROM RICHTER:
« THE SCULPTURE OF THE GREEKS ».

DOURIS (FIRST DECADES OF THE 5TH CENTURY B. C.): RED-FIGURED VASE WITH SATYRS.
BRITISH MUSEUM, LONDON.

WOMEN AT TOILET. RED-FIGURED VASE (5TH CENTURY B. C.). GLYPTOTHEK, MUNICH.

24

TWO WOMEN GOSSIPING. GREEK TERRACOTTA (3RD CENTURY B. C.). BRITISH MUSEUM, LONDON.

GERMAIN PILON (?): FOUNTAIN. MUSEUM OF FINE ARTS, BOSTON.

ALBRECHT DÜRER: ADAM. PITTI PALACE, FLORENCE.

ALBRECHT DÜRER: EVE. PITTI PALACE, FLORENCE.

PABLO PICASSO: PORTRAIT OF VOLLARD (DRAWING). METROPOLITAN MUSEUM, NEW YORK.

PABLO PICASSO: WOMAN (1938). PRIVATE COLLECTION.

POLYPHEMOS. HELLENISTIC BASRELIEF. VILLA ALBANI, ROME.

THE RAPE OF EUROPA. POMPEIAN FRESCO. NATIONAL MUSEUM, NAPLES.

ULYSSES AND THE LAESTRYGONES. FRESCO. VATICAN, ROME.

MINIATURE FROM THE MENOLOGION OF BASIL II (11TH CENTURY A. D.). VATICAN LIBRARY, ROME.

SUSANNA AND THE ELDERS. 3RD CENTURY FRESCO IN THE CATACOMBS OF PIETRO AND MARCELLINO, ROME.

KING DAVID PLAYING THE HARP. 12TH CENTURY FRESCO. ST. NICHOLAS, TAVANT (INDRE ET LOIRE).

36

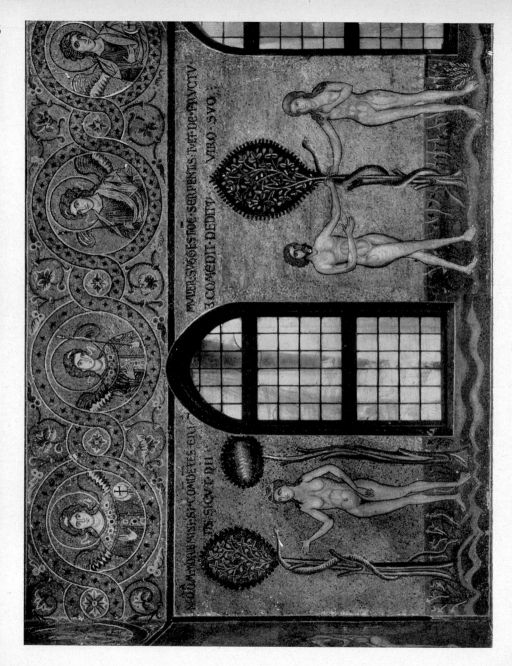

ADAM AND EVE. 12TH CENTURY MOSAIC. CATHEDRAL, MONREALE.

DETAIL FROM THE LAST JUDGEMENT. 13TH CENTURY MOSAIC. BAPTISTERY, FLORENCE.

JAN VAN EYCK (?): JONAH COMING OUT OF THE WHALE. MINIATURE FROM THE TRIVULZIO BOOK OF HOURS. MUNICIPAL MUSEUM, TURIN.

39

JAN VAN EYCK (?): THE BAPTISM OF CHRIST. MINIATURE FROM THE TRIVULZIO BOOK OF HOURS.
MUNICIPAL MUSEUM, TURIN.

JAN VAN EYCK (?): LANDING OF DUKE WILLIAM OF BAVARIA. MINIATURE FROM THE DESTROYED
TURIN BOOK OF HOURS.

JAN VAN EYCK: MADONNA AND CHANCELLOR ROLLIN (DETAIL). LOUVRE, PARIS.

42

ROGIER VAN DER WEYDEN; NATIVITY (DETAIL). KAISER FRIEDRICH MUSEUM, BERLIN.

MASTER OF THE LIFE OF THE VIRGIN: THE VISITATION WITH A DONOR (DETAIL). ALTE PINAKOTHEK, MUNICH.

HENRI MET DE BLES: THE BRONZE AGE. UFFIZI, FLORENCE.

JOACHIM PATINIER: SAINT JEROME. PRADO, MADRID.

FRA ANGELICO: DEPOSITION (DETAIL). SAN MARCO MUSEUM, FLORENCE.

FRA FILIPPO: NATIVITY (DETAIL). KAISER FRIEDRICH MUSEUM, BERLIN.

48

BALDOVINETTI: NATIVITY (DETAIL). FRESCO IN THE FORECOURT OF SS. ANNUNZIATA, FLORENCE.

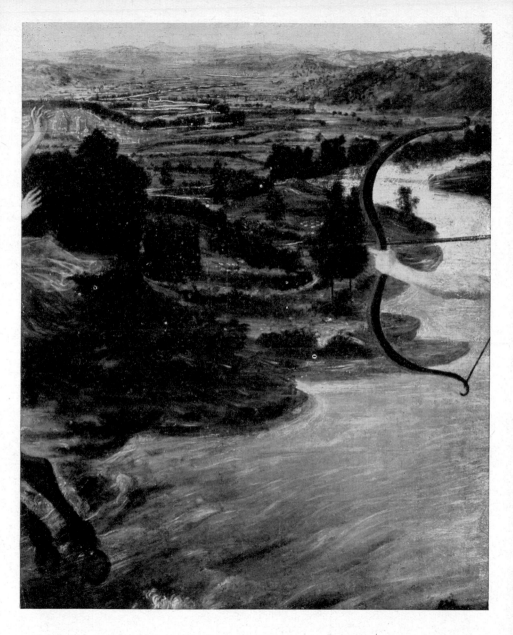

ANTONIO POLLAJUOLO: THE RAPE OF DEJANIRA (DETAIL). JARVES COLLECTION, NEW HAVEN.

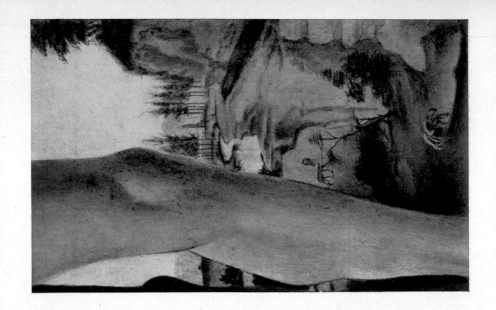

BOTTICELLI: SAINT SEBASTIAN (DETAIL). KAISER FRIEDRICH MUSEUM, BERLIN.

PERUGINO: CRUCIFIXION. FRESCO IN S. MARIA MADDALENA DE' PAZZI, FLORENCE.

RAPHAEL: SIXTINE MADONNA. GALLERY, DRESDEN.

FRA BARTOLOMEO: THE CREATION OF EVE. NATIONAL GALLERY OF ART, WASHINGTON.

PIERO DI COSIMO: PERSEUS AND ANDROMEDA (DETAIL). UFFIZI, FLORENCE.

MANTEGNA: SAINT JEROME. MUSEUM, SAO PAULO (BRAZIL).

56

ERCOLE ROBERTI: THE ARGONAUTS. MUNICIPAL GALLERY, PADUA.

FRANCESCO DEL COSSA: LEGEND OF SAINT HYACINTH (DETAIL). VATICAN GALLERY, ROME.

58

COSMÈ TURA: SAINT JEROME IN THE DESERT. NATIONAL GALLERY, LONDON.

LIBERALE DA VERONA: ADORATION OF THE MAGI. CATHEDRAL, VERONA.

GIROLAMO DA CREMONA: MINIATURE (GR. N/8). CATHEDRAL LIBRARY, SIENA.

GIOVANNI BELLINI: RESURRECTION. KAISER FRIEDRICH MUSEUM, BERLIN.

GIOVANNI BELLINI: MADONNA IN LANDSCAPE. NATIONAL GALLERY, LONDON.

GIOVANNI BELLINI: ALLEGORY. UFFIZI, FLORENCE.

GIOVANNI BELLINI (AND TITIAN): THE FEAST OF THE GODS. NATIONAL GALLERY OF ART, WASHINGTON.

GIORGIONE: « FÊTE CHAMPÊTRE ». LOUVRE, PARIS.

GIORGIONE: THE TEMPEST. ACADEMY, VENICE.

TITIAN: « NOLI ME TANGERE ». NATIONAL GALLERY, LONDON.

TITIAN: THE VENUS OF THE PARDO (DETAIL). LOUVRE, PARIS.

TITIAN: THE RAPE OF EUROPA. GARDNER MUSEUM, BOSTON.

RUBENS: LANDSCAPE WITH HARVESTERS. PITTI PALACE, FLORENCE.

SALVATOR ROSA: LANDSCAPE. FOGG ART MUSEUM, CAMBRIDGE (MASS.).

REMBRANDT: LANDSCAPE WITH OBELISK. GARDNER MUSEUM, BOSTON.

HERCULES SEGHERS: LANDSCAPE: UFFIZI, FLORENCE.

74

JAN BOTH: LANDSCAPE. NATIONAL GALLERY, LONDON.

ALBERT CUYP: CATTLE AND HORSES. NATIONAL GALLERY, LONDON.

NICOLAS POUSSIN: DIOGENES THROWS AWAY HIS DRINKING BOWL. LOUVRE, PARIS.

NICOLAS POUSSIN: ST. JOHN AT PATMOS. KAISER FRIEDRICH MUSEUM, BERLIN.

CLAUDE LORRAIN: CARLO AND UBALDO EMBARKING IN PURSUIT OF RINALDO. THIESSEN COLLECTION, LUGANO.

CLAUDE J. VERNET: BATHERS. LOUVRE, PARIS.

J. CONSTABLE: THE HAY-WAIN. NATIONAL GALLERY, LONDON.

J. CONSTABLE: WEYMOUTH BAY. NATIONAL GALLERY, LONDON.

J. S. COTMAN: CASTLE EDEN DEAN. NATIONAL GALLERY OF SCOTLAND, EDINBURGH.

J. B. C. COROT: THE GOAT-HERD. NATIONAL GALLERY OF SCOTLAND, EDINBURGH.

J. B. C. COROT: VIEW OF THE CHÂTEAU DE PIERREFONDS. MUSÉE, QUIMPER.

H. G. E. DEGAS: CARRIAGE AT RACES. MUSEUM OF FINE ARTS, BOSTON.

J. M. W. TURNER: SUNSET. MUSEUM OF FINE ARTS, CLEVELAND.

A. RENOIR: LANDSCAPE. METROPOLITAN MUSEUM, NEW YORK.

CÉZANNE: MONT ST. VICTOIRE AND VIADUCT. PRIVATE COLLECTION.